# MAKE ME THE BEST

# FOOTBALL PLAYER

BY DAN MYERS

SportsZone

An Imprint of Abdo Publishing
abdopublishing.com

**abdopublishing.com**

Published by Abdo Publishing, a division of ABDO, PO Box 398166, Minneapolis, Minnesota 55439. Copyright © 2017 by Abdo Consulting Group, Inc. International copyrights reserved in all countries. No part of this book may be reproduced in any form without written permission from the publisher. SportsZone™ is a trademark and logo of Abdo Publishing.

Printed in the United States of America, North Mankato, Minnesota
092016
012017

Cover Photos: Daniel Padavona/Shutterstock Images, top left, middle left; Shutterstock Images, bottom left; Brandon Wade/AP Images, bottom right; Christopher Futcher/ iStockphoto, top right
Interior Photos: Daniel Padavona/Shutterstock Images, 4(top), 4 (middle); Shutterstock Images, 4 (bottom); Brandon Wade/AP Images, 4–5 (bottom), 27; Christopher Futcher/ iStockphoto, 4–5 (top); Detroit Lions/AP Images, 7; David Drapkin/AP Images, 8, 40; Al Tielemans/AP Images, 11; Tom Lynn/AP Images, 13; Kevin Terrell/AP Images, 15; Paul Spinelli/AP Images, 16, 43; Tom Gannam/AP Images, 19; Gene J. Puskar/AP Images, 21; Kent Smith/AP Images, 23; Weston Kenney/AP Images, 24; Al Messerschmidt/AP Images, 29; Paul Jasienski/AP Images, 31; Gregory Bull/AP Images, 32; Peter Read Miller/AP Images, 35; Tom Hauck/AP Images, 37; Eric Christian Smith/AP Images, 38–39; Aaron M. Sprecher/AP Images, 45

Editor: Patrick Donnelly
Series Designer: Nikki Farinella
Content Consultant: Tim Triplett, veteran college football coach

**Publisher's Cataloging-in-Publication Data**

Names: Myers, Dan, author.
Title: Make me the best football player / by Dan Myers.
Description: Minneapolis, MN : Abdo Publishing, 2017. | Series: Make me the best athlete | Includes bibliographical references and index.
Identifiers: LCCN 2016945396 | ISBN 9781680784886 (lib. bdg.) | ISBN 9781680798166 (ebook)
Subjects: LCSH: Football--Juvenile literature.
Classification: DDC 796.332--dc23
LC record available at http://lccn.loc.gov/2016945396

# TABLE OF CONTENTS

# INTRODUCTION

Football is the most popular sport in the United States. Every fall, millions of people are thrilled by the long runs, the big hits, the crazy catches, and the perfect throws that National Football League (NFL) players execute in every game.

Football players put in long hours working to become the best they can be. Many players hang up their cleats for good after high school. Some go on to play college ball. The very best make it to the NFL. How did they get there? Read on to find out what it takes to become the best of the best.

# PASS LIKE

# AARON RODGERS

On December 3, 2015, the Green Bay Packers needed a miracle. It's a good thing they had Aaron Rodgers playing quarterback.

The Packers stood 61 yards from their end zone, trailing the Detroit Lions by two points. The game had come down to one final play. Rodgers made it one Packers fans would remember for the rest of their lives. He took the shotgun snap and scrambled around the backfield, giving his receivers time to get downfield. Then Rodgers stepped up to the 35-yard line and launched the ball as high and as far as he could.

Several seconds later, the pass landed in the hands of Green Bay tight end Richard Rodgers in the

///////// When he scores a touchdown, Rodgers celebrates by putting on an imaginary wrestling championship belt.

Aaron Rodgers lofts the ball high as he throws his last-gasp pass to beat the Detroit Lions.

7

end zone. The Packers, because of a perfect throw by Aaron Rodgers, had won the game.

Green Bay selected Rodgers in the first round of the 2005 NFL Draft. After two outstanding seasons at the University of California, Berkeley, many people thought he would be among the top five draft picks. Instead, he

## PASS LIKE AARON RODGERS

- Watch your step. Clean footwork, including stepping into a throw, is just as important as arm strength.

- Find the laces. Your fingers should be on the laces of the ball. Make sure the ball fits comfortably in your hand.

- Raise it up. A good throwing motion begins by pulling the ball behind your ear and bending your elbow. Rotate your hips to get more strength behind your pass.

- Go over the top. Throw the ball with an overhand motion. This will create a more accurate throw with a tighter spiral.

- Stay in throwing position. You never know when the perfect window will open to hit a receiver. You need to be ready to throw at all times.

Rodgers steps into a throw in Green Bay's Super Bowl victory over Pittsburgh.

slipped to 24th overall. Rodgers was disappointed, but the Packers were thrilled to get such a great talent.

Since taking over the starting position from Brett Favre in 2008, Rodgers has been piling up awards. He was named the Most Valuable Player (MVP) of the Super Bowl after leading Green Bay to a 31–25 victory over the Pittsburgh Steelers following the 2010 season. Rodgers earned NFL MVP honors in 2011 and 2014.

The quarterback is usually considered the most important position on the field. He handles the football on

## DAN MARINO

When Dan Marino retired in 2000, the former Miami Dolphins quarterback held almost every NFL career passing record. With his lightning-quick release and powerful arm, Marino retired with the most touchdowns, completions, attempts, and yards in a career. He also held the record for most passing yards and touchdowns in one season.

Rodgers takes charge on the field by calling out defensive alignments and changing plays.

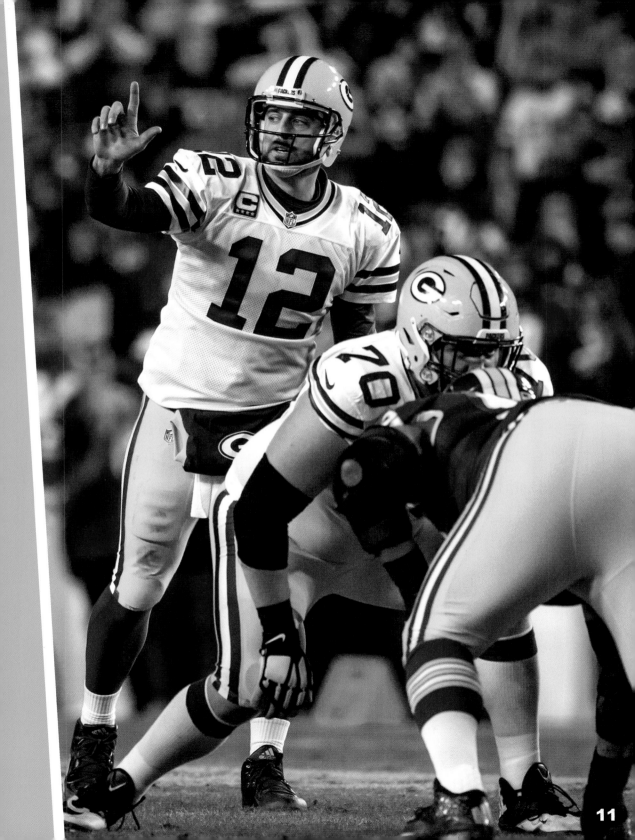

every down. The quarterback also is thought of as a coach on the field. Quarterbacks need to know where every player is lined up and where they are going on every play.

Rodgers is one of the most skilled quarterbacks in the NFL. He is an accurate passer but is also athletic enough to keep the ball and run with it. He also takes care of the football by not throwing many interceptions. From 2011 to 2015, he threw 170 touchdown passes and was intercepted just 33 times.

Passing is an important part of football, and NFL teams are passing more than they ever have in the past. The best teams are built around quarterbacks such as Rodgers, who can lead an offense quickly down the field and put up lots of points. Accuracy, arm strength, leadership, and smarts all make for a great quarterback. Hard work and tremendous talent helped Rodgers develop all of these skills.

California went 18–8 in the regular season and split two bowl games during Rodgers's two years as a starter.

## DRILL DOWN!

This exercise will help you perfect your throwing motion.

1. Stand on the goal line with your partner 10 yards behind the end line.

2. Take turns throwing the ball over the crossbar to each other. Try to keep the ball as close to the crossbar as possible without hitting it.

3. You can incorporate a five-step drop before throwing. Or roll to the right or left and throw on the run.

4. A soccer goal or high fence can be used in place of goalposts.

# RUN LIKE
# LE'VEON BELL

The easiest way for an offense to move the ball forward is to hand it to a great running back. Since entering the NFL in 2013, Pittsburgh Steelers running back Le'Veon Bell has become one of the best in the league at his position.

Bell wasn't a major recruit out of high school in Groveport, Ohio. Unlike some players, he didn't announce his college selection by putting on a school hat on national television. In fact, most big schools did not recruit him. Then his high school coach called an old friend, Michigan State University football coach Mark Dantonio.

Bell also participated in track and field in high school. He was an outstanding high jumper.

Le'Veon Bell uses his speed to outrun defenders.

Dantonio sent an assistant coach to watch Bell play basketball. Bell played many sports in high school and did well in football, basketball, and track and field. The coach saw what a great athlete Bell was and determined he could be a good college football player. The Spartans offered Bell a scholarship, and he accepted.

## RUN LIKE LE'VEON BELL

- Know your assignment. Are you carrying the ball, blocking, or running a pass route? Running backs have a variety of responsibilities depending on the play.

- Study. If you're carrying the ball, know where your hole is supposed to be. Understand why the linemen in front of you are blocking the way they are. It will make your job easier.

- Move your feet. Great running backs are always finding ways to make themselves faster. This starts in offseason training and continues in practice during the week.

- Maintain ball security. Keep five points of contact with the football—fingertip, forearm, bicep, chest, and palm. A firm, stable grip will make it difficult for an opponent to rip the ball away.

Great vision and quick feet help Bell avoid tackles.

In his final year at Michigan State, Bell led all major-college running backs with 382 carries.

Bell was good enough to get some playing time as a freshman before leading the Spartans in rushing as a sophomore. When he was a junior, Bell rushed for an eye-popping 1,793 yards in 13 games. He decided to skip his senior year and entered the 2013 NFL Draft. The Steelers picked him in the second round.

Bell quickly showed that he had the speed to outrun all levels of a defense. But he also showed an important trait

## BARRY SANDERS

Defenders had a hard time keeping tabs on Barry Sanders. One of the most electrifying players of his era, the Detroit Lions running back used shifty moves and breakaway speed to keep space between him and his opponents. Sanders rushed for 15,269 yards during his 10-year NFL career. He was second on the career rushing yards list when he retired in 1999. Despite being a flashy runner, Sanders was humble on the field. When he scored, he simply handed the ball to an official after he reached the end zone.

Bell beats opponents by catching passes out of the backfield.

that's rarely found in young running backs. He was good
at being patient.

When a quarterback takes the snap and turns to hand
the ball to the running back, the offensive line in front
of him might take a second or two to open up a hole.
Good running backs can find a small hole and gain five
or six yards on a play. Great ones such as Bell trust their
blockers and wait an extra half second for a small hole
to turn into a big one. That patience gives Bell a chance
to hit the hole at full speed and turn a solid gain into a
game-breaking run.

Since entering the league, Bell has also become one
of the best receiving running backs in the NFL. With
teams running less and passing more, Bell made himself
a valuable receiver out of the
backfield. After catching 45 passes
as a rookie, Bell caught 83 passes
in his second season for more than
800 yards and three touchdowns.

**Bell made his NFL debut in London, England. The Steelers faced the Minnesota Vikings there on September 29, 2013.**

# DRILL DOWN!

Develop quick feet with this version of the classic tire drill.

1.  Set ropes on the ground in a 2x5 grid. If you don't have ropes, use the lines on the field as a guide.

2.  Keeping your knees high, move through the grid while stepping one foot into each box.

3.  Increase your speed as you become more comfortable with the movement.

4.  Carry a ball high and tight and keep your eyes up to simulate on-field action.

# CATCH LIKE

# JULIO JONES

**W**ide receivers come in many different forms. Some are considered possession receivers. They have great hands but not blazing speed. Others run precise routes. And some can zoom past the defense and get open for a deep ball. Atlanta Falcons wide receiver Julio Jones is one of the rare players who can do it all.

Born and raised in the small town of Foley, Alabama, Jones earned a scholarship to the University of Alabama. Within two years, he was one of the best college receivers in the nation. He caught 78 passes for 1,133 yards and seven touchdowns that year. He declared himself eligible for the NFL Draft in 2011, and the Falcons immediately

**After his rookie season, Jones cut his long hair and donated it to a charity that makes wigs for children with cancer.**

Julio Jones leaps over Panthers linebacker Luke Kuechly to make an amazing catch in 2015.

showed how much they wanted him. The team traded away five draft picks to move up to the sixth overall pick in the draft. They used that selection to draft Jones. He made their decision look good, scoring eight touchdowns and catching

As a college player, Jones helped Alabama go undefeated and win the national title in 2009.

## CATCH LIKE JULIO JONES

- Know your route. Running the correct pattern is a vital skill for a receiver. A receiver needs to be exactly where the quarterback expects him to be.

- Watch the ball. Follow it into your hands and then your body. Don't look up field until the ball is secure.

- Keep your hands soft. Balls bounce off rigid targets. Let the ball move your hands toward your body as you catch it.

- Mind your fingers. If the ball is below your waist, keep your pinkies together as you catch it. If the ball is above your waist, put your thumbs together so your hands form a W.

- Know the situation. On third down, run your route past the line to gain so you can come back to the ball and still get a first down. Watch the defense to see how you'll be covered.

Concentration is key for a receiver, especially when a defender is trying to knock the ball away.

54 passes for 959 yards as a rookie, despite missing three games.

Jones has skills that set him apart in the NFL. He rarely drops passes, displaying the reliable hands a quarterback looks for in a target. He has game-breaking speed to run away from defenders once he has the ball in his hands. But Jones also studies other teams' defenses

In 2015 Jones posted 1,871 receiving yards, the second-most for one season in NFL history.

## JERRY RICE

Jerry Rice is often called the greatest wide receiver of all time. But he began his career in the NFL with a lot to prove. He was a first-round pick of the San Francisco 49ers in 1985, but he didn't face great competition at tiny Mississippi Valley State University. He also didn't have top-end speed. But Rice worked hard to become great. He improved his speed and footwork while also becoming one of the most reliable targets in the league. In 20 NFL seasons, Rice set almost every career receiving record, including catches, yards, and touchdowns.

Jones demonstrates the importance of looking the ball into your hands when making a catch.

and learns where he can take advantage of holes in their pass coverage.

Receivers need to anticipate what they'll see from a defense. Will they try to cover you one-on-one—also known as man coverage? Or will the defenders cover areas of the field, also called zone coverage? Jones uses his skills to defeat both. He's bigger and stronger than most cornerbacks who try to cover him by themselves. He's also smart enough to find the soft spots in a zone defense and get open for his quarterback.

In high school Jones was the Alabama state champion in the long jump and the triple jump twice. He also won the state title in the high jump and finished second in the 100-meter dash.

## DRILL DOWN!

The Clock Drill will help you catch the ball wherever it's thrown.

1.  Playing catch with a teammate, start by throwing it straight above his head (or 12 on a clock face).

2.  Move around in a circle, practicing catches at different spots on the "clock."

3.  Always catch and tuck the ball away before throwing it back.

4.  Add movement by catching the ball at different points of the clock while on the run.

# TACKLE LIKE

# LUKE KUECHLY

Quarterbacks should know where every player on offense is supposed to go on each play. Which routes will a receiver run? What hole is the running back supposed to hit? What kind of blocking is his offensive line giving him?

The middle linebacker is like the quarterback of the defense. And Luke Kuechly of the Carolina Panthers is one of the best middle linebackers in the NFL.

**Kuechly made 24 tackles—one shy of the NFL record—in a 2013 game against the New Orleans Saints.**

On running plays, Kuechly's job is to find the football and plug the hole, tackling an offensive running back before he can get a big gain. If the play is a pass, Kuechly might cover a tight end over the middle or a running back on a pass pattern out of the

**Luke Kuechly calls out instructions to his Carolina Panthers teammates.**

backfield. Or Kuechly might blitz to put pressure on the quarterback. No matter what teams try to do to block him, it's hard to keep Kuechly away from the football.

Kuechly is one of the best players in the NFL, but it took him years of work and overcoming disappointment

## TACKLE LIKE LUKE KUECHLY

- Study. The best defensive players are prepared for what an opponent might do. Defense is largely reactionary, because offensive players know where they are going on every play. Getting a feel for their tendencies will help you react faster.

- Keep your head up. You have to see what you're hitting. If you're looking at the ground when making contact, you're increasing the risk of serious injury. You also might miss the tackle.

- Wrap up. You don't get extra points by going for the big highlight-reel hit—you just risk letting your opponent bounce off you and keep gaining yards. Wrap up your target and bring him to the ground.

- Move your feet. Keep your feet active once you make contact. Offensive players use their size and speed to drag a tackler who has simply latched on to them.

Kuechly flattens Denver's Demaryius Thomas during Super Bowl 50.

to get there. Growing up in Cincinnati, Kuechly played offensive line and linebacker. He wanted to play just defense, although he was willing to do what was best for the team. As a junior, he led St. Xavier High School to a state championship while playing outside linebacker. When he was a senior, the coaches made him the focus of their defense, and he excelled.

When he began getting college scholarship offers, Kuechly dreamed of playing for a big program such as Ohio State or Notre Dame, but neither school showed

## RAY LEWIS

Ray Lewis was considered too small to play in the NFL by some coaches and general managers. The Baltimore Ravens took him with the 26th pick of the 1996 NFL Draft. It's safe to say he made a few teams regret not picking him. A 13-time Pro Bowl player, Lewis won the NFL's Defensive Player of the Year Award twice and also led Baltimore to two Super Bowl championships before retiring in 2012.

Kuechly displays his strong tackling skills as he wraps up Broncos running back C. J. Anderson.

much interest in him. People told him he was too small to play major college football.

Kuechly chose to go to Boston College and quickly became one of the best players in the country. Over three years with the Eagles, Kuechly set a record with 33 consecutive games with at least 10 tackles. Carolina selected him with the ninth pick in the 2012 draft, and the success he had in college immediately translated to the NFL.

Kuechly returned two interceptions for touchdowns in the 2015 NFL Playoffs.

With the growing emphasis on the passing game, Kuechly's ability to cover as well as tackle has become more valuable. He didn't know it at the time, but the all-around skills Kuechly developed as a kid have helped him thrive as a linebacker in today's NFL.

# DRILL DOWN!

Develop agility and practice changing directions with this drill.

1. Line up five cones five yards apart in the shape of an M.

2. Start in the bottom-left corner of the M. Run to the second cone. Once there, run backward to the third cone.

3. Continue through all five cones, keeping your head and eyes up. Once finished, repeat the process in reverse.

4. Repeat while shuffling your feet, focusing on staying low to the ground with a wide base and keeping your shoulders square to the front while moving.

# PASS RUSH LIKE

# J. J. WATT

It's third down and six yards to go. It's late in the game, and the offense needs a touchdown to win. The quarterback takes the snap and drops back to pass. He's looking downfield for an open receiver when Houston Texans defensive end J. J. Watt spins around the offensive tackle and charges at him.

The quarterback doesn't see Watt coming. He gets hit, goes down hard, and fumbles the football. Watt scoops it up, and the Texans hold on to win the game.

Watt runs the Justin J. Watt Foundation, which gives money to middle schools around the country to fund after-school activities for kids.

Few plays are more exciting than a big quarterback sack, and Watt makes plenty of them as one of the NFL's top defensive players.

J. J. Watt knows that a big quarterback sack can fire up the defense.

But Watt wasn't always a dominant defensive player. If some colleges had gotten their way, Watt might be playing offense instead.

It's hard to believe that Watt, one of the most feared defensive ends in the NFL, began his college

As an NFL rookie, Watt returned an interception 29 yards for a touchdown in a playoff game against the Cincinnati Bengals.

## BLITZ LIKE J. J. WATT

- Use your hands. Although offensive linemen get flagged for holding your jersey, you can grab theirs legally to create leverage and gain an advantage in a one-on-one battle.

- Read the clues. An offensive lineman might tip off which direction the play is going by how he blocks. Which direction is he shielding a defensive player? Chances are, that's a tip to where the play is headed. Learn to read how a lineman is blocking and your job becomes easier.

- Know your assignment. Defensive linemen must know where to line up and what their responsibilities are on every play. Are you supposed to hit an inside gap or go outside? Are you supposed to play the run or the pass? Knowing your job and where to line up is half the battle.

Watt is a defensive end, but he's quick enough to pressure the quarterback up the middle.

career as a tight end at Central Michigan University. His coaches told him they wanted him to score touchdowns and be a difference-maker on offense. But Watt caught just eight passes for 77 yards in 14 games as a freshman. After the season, his coaches wanted to move him to the offensive line.

Watt wasn't interested. Instead, he gave up his scholarship to transfer to the University of Wisconsin,

## REGGIE WHITE

Off the field, Reggie White was an ordained Baptist minister. On the field, White was known as the "Minister of Defense." One of the best defensive players in NFL history, White had 198 sacks during his 15-year NFL career. That's the second-most in NFL history behind Bruce Smith, who needed four more seasons to pass White by just two sacks. White went to 13 consecutive Pro Bowls with the Philadelphia Eagles and Green Bay Packers and was twice named the NFL's Defensive Player of the Year. He was inducted into the Pro Football Hall of Fame in 2006.

Offensive linemen have their hands full trying to keep Watt out of the backfield.

where he walked on as a defensive end. That turned out to be a wise choice.

At Wisconsin Watt worked hard at his craft, grew into his body, and became a star. After two seasons he decided to enter the NFL Draft. The Texans took him with the 11th overall pick in 2011.

A good pass rush can help cover for a defense with shaky pass coverage. When the opposing quarterback is always on the run, he can't look downfield and find open receivers. Even if a defensive line doesn't get the sack, consistent pressure can force rushed throws and hasty decisions. Watt uses his quickness to dart past offensive linemen, his size to overpower blockers, and his speed to chase down the quarterback.

Few players work harder in the weight room than Watt, who weighed 240 pounds as a college freshman. By the time he was ready for the NFL, Watt had gained nearly 50 pounds of muscle. Lifting weights and eating right helped Watt become a better football player.

## DRILL DOWN!

This drill will help you keep an offensive lineman's hands in check.

1. Stand facing a teammate no more than arm's length apart.

2. Without moving his feet, the offensive player attempts to hit or grab the defensive player's chest, shoulders, or arms with one or both hands.

3. The defensive player must react and knock his opponent's hands away, also without moving his feet.

4. Younger players should concentrate on knocking the hands away. Older players can mix in more advanced techniques.

# GLOSSARY

### BLITZ

When a linebacker or defensive back attacks the line of scrimmage to stop a run or sack the quarterback.

### FUMBLE

When a player with the ball loses possession, allowing the opponent a chance to recover it.

### GOAL LINE

The edge of the end zone that a player must cross with the ball to score a touchdown.

### INTERCEPTION

When a defensive player catches a pass intended for an offensive player.

### LINE OF SCRIMMAGE

The place on the field where a play starts.

### SACK

A tackle of the quarterback behind the line of scrimmage before he can pass the ball.

### SCHOLARSHIP

Money given to a student to pay for education expenses.

### SCRAMBLE

To run around with the ball behind the line of scrimmage while looking for an open receiver.

### SHOTGUN

A formation in which the quarterback lines up three to five yards behind the center and takes the snap in the air.

### SNAP

The start of each play, when the center hikes the ball between his legs to a player behind him, usually the quarterback.

# FOR MORE INFORMATION

## BOOKS

Anderson, Jameson. *Aaron Rodgers*. Minneapolis, MN: Abdo Publishing, 2015.

Scheff, Matt. *J. J. Watt*. Minneapolis, MN: Abdo Publishing, 2016.

Wilner, Barry. *The Best NFL Receivers of All Time*. Minneapolis, MN: Abdo Publishing, 2014.

## WEBSITES

To learn more about football, visit **booklinks.abdopublishing.com**. These links are routinely monitored and updated to provide the most current information available.

## PLACE TO VISIT

**Pro Football Hall of Fame**
2121 George Halas Drive NW
Canton, Ohio 44708
(330) 456-8207
http://www.profootballhof.com
Built in 1963, the Pro Football Hall of Fame celebrates the best football players ever to play the game. Up to seven inductees are enshrined each year. The purpose of the hall is to honor the heroes of the game, preserve its history, promote its values, and celebrate its excellence.

# INDEX

# ABOUT THE AUTHOR

Dan Myers was raised in Eagan, Minnesota, and graduated with a degree in journalism from Minnesota State University. He has covered sports at all levels in the Twin Cities since 2008. He and his wife live in Hudson, Wisconsin, with their beagle, Kato.